Gun Control and the Right to Bear Arms

Barbara Long

Enslow Publishers, Inc.

40 Industrial Road	PO Box 38
Box 398	Aldershot
Berkeley Heights, NJ 07922	Hants GU12 6BP
USA	UK

http://www.enslow.com

Library of Congress Cataloging-in-Publication Data

Long, Barbara, 1954–
    Gun control and the right to bear arms : a pro/con issue / Barbara
Long.
        v. cm. — (Hot pro/con issues)
    Includes bibliographical references and index.
    Contents: Youth and guns—The history of gun use—Regulation of gun
ownership and use—Arguments in favor of gun control—Arguments
against gun control — Gun control in the twenty-first century.
    ISBN 0-7660-1819-9 (hardcover)
    1. Gun control—United States—Juvenile literature. [1. Gun control.]
I. Title. II. Series.
HV7436 .L66 2002
363.3'3'0973—dc21
                                        2002000388

Printed in the United States of America

10 9 8 7 6 5 4 3 2 1

To Our Readers: We have done our best to make sure all Internet Addresses in
this book were active and appropriate when we went to press. However, the
author and the publisher have no control over and assume no liability for the
material available on those Internet sites or on other Web sites they may link to.
Any comments or suggestions can be sent by e-mail to comments@enslow.com
or to the address on the back cover.

Illustration Credits: AP/Wide World, pp. 7, 8, 30, 32, 35, 54; Corbis
Images Royalty-Free, pp. 4, 13; Corel Corporation, pp. 1, 14, 16, 17;
National Archives, pp. 22, 25; Painet Stock Photos, pp. 19, 41, 45, 52.

Cover Illustration: Corbis Images Royalty-Free.

Contents

Chapter 1

Youths and Guns

On Monday, March 5, 2001, students entered Santana High School in Santee, a suburb of San Diego, California. They expected the day to be just like any other. Instead, at 9:20 A.M., the routine day turned violent. As the school's nineteen hundred pupils began to change from their first-period to second-period classes, students in one hallway heard several loud pops.

"I thought it was firecrackers but it wasn't," said Amy Barney, a student at the school.[1]

Another pupil, Alicia Zimmer, said, "It sounded more like a cap gun than anything."[2]

Surprise and disbelief turned to panic as students realized that someone was shooting real bullets. Without warning, hundreds of students had become moving targets for Charles Andrew "Andy" Williams. The fifteen-year-old ninth grader had loaded a handgun in the boys' restroom and started shooting from the bathroom's doorway.

Zimmer described her view of the scene: "I was probably about ten feet away from a couple of the victims . . . it was in the middle of the hall, the small quad . . . I saw a victim, a boy, laying on the floor, with his face downward. There was another girl standing there with blood all over her arms." She added, "It was really scary. Everybody was running. A whole lot of people were crying."[3]

"I didn't see where the shots were coming at first, and then you looked over and you see the kid smiling and shooting his weapon," student John Sharp told news media. "When he came back out of the bathroom, he was smiling. He was looking around and smiling. With his weapon, he fired two more shots and went back in."[4] Williams stayed in the restroom, where he was arrested by an off-duty police officer. He dropped his gun and told the officers that he acted alone, saying, "It's only me."[5]

Williams was quickly taken into custody. In this short time, though, he killed two students—seventeen-year-old Randy Gordon and fourteen-year-old Brian Zuckor. His shooting also wounded thirteen others, including fellow students, an unarmed school security guard, and a twenty-nine-year-old student teacher. And his violent act left many people looking for answers to a school problem that concerns teachers, students, parents, and society at large.

In Santee, investigators searched for reasons why Williams would try to kill his fellow classmates. Apparently, Williams was unhappy about moving with his father from Maryland to California the summer before. In a videotape Williams made before the shootings, shown later on the television news magazine show *Inside Edition*, Williams said, "My school is horrible. I hate it there. Everyone is all nice to me there 'cause they're stupid. I really don't like my school. I wish I lived back in Maryland."[6]

More School Shootings and Violent Threats Occur

On Wednesday of that same week in March 2001, fourteen-year-old Elizabeth Catherine Bush took a loaded gun into the cafeteria of Bishop Neumann Junior-Senior

*S*tudents from Santana High School in Santee, California, comfort each other after a shooting at their school on March 5, 2001.

High School in Williamsport, Pennsylvania. Williamsport, about 160 miles northwest of Philadelphia, is home of baseball's Little League World Series. Bush entered the cafeteria, where about half of the school's 230 students were eating lunch. Bush fired the gun, shooting thirteen-year-old Kimberly Marchese in the right shoulder. After being shot, Marchese ran from the cafeteria along with other frightened students.

A freshman student, fourteen-year-old Brent Paucke, and two school administrators talked Bush into dropping the gun. Paucke kicked away the gun, and Bush was taken into custody.

The shooter and the victim knew each other. According to Tom Marino, the county district attorney, there was "some kind of friction between them."[7]

*S*antana High School shooting suspect Andy Williams is shown at his arraignment flanked by his public defenders: Jo Pastore, left, and Randy Mize, right.

During that fateful week in 2001, there were more incidents of guns at school. On Monday, the same day as the Santana High School shootings, an eight-year-old boy threatened to shoot a student at the Henry C. Lea School in West Philadelphia, Pennsylvania.

"He said he's going to shoot me," Fatimah Edwards told authorities. She added, "He said he's going to make it a bloodbath and throw me in the Dumpster."[8] The boy was taken into custody before he could act. Police officers found a pistol and ammunition in his backpack.

On Tuesday, March 6, 2001, a twelve-year-old student at the Thomas Morton Elementary School in Southwest Philadelphia was arrested for having a pistol. He had argued with another boy and came to school with the firearm.

Also on Tuesday, a fifteen-year-old freshman at Camden High School in New Jersey was charged with threatening to shoot a group of students who had teased him. The boy promised to return with a gun, but police officers picked him up at his home and no weapon was found.

On Wednesday, twenty-year-old James Johansen, a former student at Frankford High in Philadelphia, was arrested. He had threatened to shoot a student and a teacher at the high school during a conversation in an Internet chat room. An off-duty police officer spotted the threat by chance. The officer quickly alerted Northeast Philadelphia detectives, who arrested Johansen and charged him with making threats of terrorism, recklessly endangering another person, and possessing an instrument of crime.[9]

It is important to note that in these last four incidents, violence was prevented by the responsible actions of both students and authorities. Because people quickly reported and responded to the violent threats, injury—and possibly death—was prevented.

Irresponsible Gun Use

The school gun shootings and threats you just read about happened during one week out of one year. Clearly, the combination of youths and guns can be very dangerous. The combination can also lead to tragic deaths. The deadliest school shooting to date occurred at Columbine High School in Littleton, Colorado. In a tragedy covered in detail by the media, two teenaged boys fatally shot a teacher and twelve fellow students at the school before taking their own lives on April 20, 1999.

Although incidents of school gun violence continue to make the news, schools are not the only place where young people are killed by guns. Gun violence has become all too common on American streets and in American homes. In 1998, more than ten children and teenagers, ages nineteen and under, were killed with guns every day.[10] The following chart offers a breakdown of the total 30,708 Americans who died from guns in 1998.[11]

1998 Gun-Related Deaths in the United States		
Cause	Number	Percentage of total
Murder	12,102	39%
Suicide	17,424	57%
Accident	866	3%
Unknown intent	316	1%

Over the years good news has emerged. During the 1990s, gun-related deaths in the United States dropped 26 percent to the lowest level since 1966.[12]

The following table shows results from a study by the Centers for Disease Control and Prevention.[13]

Drop in Gun-Related Deaths		
Year	Number of Gun-Related Deaths	Death rate per 100,000 people
1993	39,595	15.4
1998	30,708	11.4

The bad news is that, even with the decline in gun-related deaths, an average of 265 people a day were shot in 1997.[14] In addition, guns remain the second leading cause of injury-related deaths in the United States, trailing only car-related deaths.[15]

Accidental Shootings

Gun injury and death have happened and can happen in many places—schools, restaurants, streets, and homes. Many young people die or are injured right in their own home after finding and playing with a loaded gun.

The following accidental shootings are two tragic examples.

In early July 2001 in the Bronx, New York, nine-year-old Taniqua Hall reached on top of a cabinet for a jar of peanut butter to make a sandwich. Instead, she picked up a handgun and accidentally shot herself in the chest. She died a short time later.

Deputy Police Chief Joseph J. Reznick was the commander of the Bronx detectives who investigated the accidental shooting. He said, "This is one of those horror stories when you have that combination of kids and guns. It's every parent's worst nightmare."[16]

On September 15, 2001, a three-year-old boy in Spotsylvania County, Virginia, shot and killed himself with a gun his father had brought into the house for protection in the wake of the September 11 terrorist attacks.[17]

The accidental shooting of any person, indeed, is a nightmare for all those involved. Guns must be carefully stored and handled so as not to cause accidental injury or death to family and friends.

Suicides

Suicide is the eighth leading cause of death for all Americans. For young people between fifteen and twenty-four years old, it is the third leading cause of death, behind accidental injury and homicide.[18] In 1998, nearly three of every five suicides, or 57 percent, were committed with a gun.[19]

In addition, a report published in 2001 indicated that guns increase the risk of suicide.[20] The table on page 12 shows the results from this study.

As shown, the risk of suicide increases fivefold when a gun is in the home. If the gun is unlocked, the suicide risk increases times six. And if the gun is loaded, the risk increases times nine.

The connection of guns to suicide risk is a cause for concern. Some people believe that access to guns needs to be more tightly controlled. In fact, access to guns has been debated for many decades.

Increased Risk of Suicide	
Access to gun	**Suicide risk multiplied**
Gun in home	By 5 times
Unlocked gun in home	By 6 times
Loaded gun in home	By 9 times

Controlling Access to Guns

In the 1960s, the assassinations of three important political leaders—John F. Kennedy, Martin Luther King, Jr., and Robert F. Kennedy—drew the public's attention to irresponsible gun use and violence. The public's outcry helped pass the first federal gun control legislation since the 1930s.

For many years, the U.S. murder rate has been four to eight times higher than that of Northern European countries and more than ten times higher than Japan's rate.[21] Some people think that the United States has a high murder rate because weak gun control laws allow easy access to guns.

In light of the growing problem of gun-related violence, especially in cases that involve children, some people would like to strictly control the ownership and use of firearms. In fact, many Americans—both pro- and anti-gun supporters—believe that commonsense gun control is necessary to help reduce violent crime and prevent accidental deaths.

Responsible Gun Use

Throughout history, guns have been used responsibly for survival and for sport. In numerous situations, firearms have been used safely for hunting game and for target-shooting activities.

As of 1999, there were about 15 million American hunters.[22] Hunting is a sport enjoyed by many Americans, and some believe that managed hunting helps maintain a balance among many species and their habitats.

Guns also have been used for self-defense to protect people from death, serious injury, or loss of property. The next paragraph describes one man who used a gun to defend his restaurant from being robbed, and possibly from being shot himself.

On January 16, 2001, Spiro Poulos was in his pizzeria in Cumberland County, Tennessee. Two armed robbers, wearing ski masks, entered the restaurant and held a gun to his head. When the robbers demanded money, Poulos reached for his own gun and fired four times. One of the robbers was hit, and the other fled. According to the police involved with the case, Poulos acted in self-defense.[23]

The Hot Topic of Guns

Estimates put the number of guns in the United States between 193 million and 250 million—almost one gun for

*O*ne study showed that access to guns in the home increases the risk of suicide anywhere from five to nine times, depending on whether the gun is locked or unlocked, loaded or unloaded.

every man, woman, and child in the country.[24] The sale and use of guns is a hot topic of debate. With each report of a death or injury resulting from gun use—especially those that involve children—the gun control debate grows hotter.

Since the birth of the nation, many Americans have owned guns. As the nation grew, gun restrictions were added, mainly at the state and local level. Then, as gun violence rose, the federal government began to pass gun control laws. Should there be restrictions on the ownership and use of firearms? Do Americans have a constitutional right to own and carry firearms?

These are some of the questions being argued during the current debate on guns. The best way to answer such difficult questions is to examine both sides of the issue.

*A*s the sun rises, a deer hunter awaits the opening day of hunting season. Throughout the history of the United States, people have used guns for hunting.

Chapter 2

The History of Gun Use

The invention of black powder, or gunpowder, is traced to China during the thirteenth century. From there, through trade and travel contacts, gunpowder became known in Europe. People soon discovered that gunpowder could be used to fire objects through the air. This use of gunpowder quickly spread throughout Asia and Europe. The first cannon was used in warfare around 1350. Eventually, such deadly power became easier to transport in the form of guns. By the middle of the sixteenth century, firearms were fairly common in Europe.

Gun Terminology

Guns are weapons that fire a bullet, a shell, or other object through the air. The *caliber* of a gun is the diameter of its barrel, and it is measured in inches, such as .32 or .45 caliber. Guns are grouped into categories by size.

For example, handguns have a short barrel through which the ammunition passes after being fired. These guns are small enough to be held in a person's hand. *Pistols* are handguns that are accurate only at short ranges. *Revolvers* are handguns with a revolving cylinder that allows the gun to be fired repeatedly.

Rifles, or long guns, have an extended barrel that is thick and heavy. All long guns have grooved barrels, called rifling, which make bullets spiral and fly in straight lines for better accuracy. With their long barrels, *shotguns* look like rifles. However, the shotgun barrel has a thin wall, and its opening is larger than that of a rifle barrel. Both the rifle and the shotgun are used for long-range shooting.

Semiautomatic guns fire one bullet each time the trigger is pulled. *Fully automatic* weapons fire continuously when the trigger is pulled. Portable automatic weapons that can fire hundreds to thousands of rounds of ammunition per minute are called *machine guns*. *Assault guns* are semiautomatic and fully automatic weapons that are used for military purposes.

The guns described above are small arms. Large arms make up another category of guns and are referred to as *cannon* or *artillery*. They are common weapons in warfare and are not part of the gun control debate.

*T*he Western Rodgers & Spencer is a 9-mm single-action blank revolver with a revolving cylinder that allows the gun to be fired repeatedly.

*T*he Colt 1911 MKIV, Series 70, is a .45 caliber semiautomatic pistol. It can fire a bullet each time the trigger is pulled.

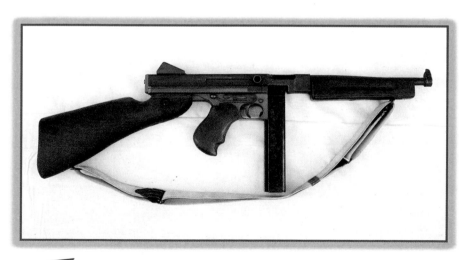

*T*he U.S. Thompson .45 caliber submachine gun features continuous fire when the trigger is pulled.

Guns and Survival

During the 1500s, gunpowder and guns changed the social fabric of European life. The new weapons tipped the balance of social and political power. Guns meant that a knight's armor was no longer invincible. Also, castles and forts were no longer impossible to attack, as these strongholds could now be destroyed by cannon assaults.

The rifle was first invented in the 1500s. This weapon became popular with soldiers, hunters, and colonists. Early American settlers carried muskets, or heavy long guns. These early guns were not very accurate, and each shot took several minutes to load. Still, they were important survival tools in a new and uncharted land, particularly for hunting game to eat.

The first American gun was the Kentucky flintlock rifle, also known as the American rifle. Daniel Boone was one famous frontiersman who used this rifle. Besides survival, settlers living in the American Colonies soon found another need for owning and using guns.

Guns and Liberty

When it came time to fight for independence from Great Britain, guns became very important. To the colonists resisting the oppression of the British royal crown, guns were a way to achieve liberty. As soldiers were needed to fight the British, workers such as farmers and blacksmiths exchanged their tools of trade for tools of war. These ordinary colonists were called Minutemen because they would pick up their guns and fight on very short notice. Minutemen played an important role in winning liberty from Great Britain.

As the new country charted its course in the late 1700s, it debated the need for having armed citizens ready to fight in a war. Some people wanted state governments to continue to train citizens for battle and provide them with arms. Others were worried that armed

*G*uns became very important to the colonists who were resisting the oppression of the English monarchy. Shown here is a Revolutionary War reenactment.

citizens could rise against the government and overthrow it. In fact, one newly formed state did face an armed rebellion of angry citizens.

Massachusetts farmers who could not pay their debts revolted against the state in 1786 and 1787. These farmers opposed the taxes and court fees that the state charged them. Daniel Shays, who had served the country in the Revolutionary War, was the farmers' leader. His armed troops forced courts in various towns to close. Since many of the rebel troops were members of the country's militia, the state of Massachusetts raised its own army to counter the armed uprisings.

On January 25, 1787, the rebels attacked the state army at the Springfield arsenal, or military storehouse.

Four farmers were killed and twenty were wounded as the state army routed Shays' forces. Although Shays' Rebellion was finally put down a week later, it raised some fears about armed citizens. Somehow the Founding Fathers of the United States needed to balance power between the government and the people.

Delegates at the Constitutional Convention held in Philadelphia in 1787 carefully crafted a document that would guide the country for centuries to come. The representatives added ten amendments to the original U.S. Constitution that they wrote. These men wanted to preserve liberty without creating lawlessness and chaos.

The Second Amendment to the U.S. Constitution recognized the need for militias in preserving the country's security. It allowed for people to keep and bear arms. Nearly two centuries later, Americans would begin to debate exactly what rights this amendment guaranteed. In the meantime, however, people freely manufactured, carried, and used firearms as they expanded America's borders.

In 1811, John Hall invented a rifle that loaded through a chamber at the back of the barrel rather than through the muzzle, or the end of the gun from which bullets are shot. Hall mass-produced these rifles using assembly lines. The Hall rifles were the first firearms with fully inter-changeable parts, which were made by machines. Because machines made the gun parts uniform, one part was easily exchanged with another. Although the U.S. Army did not use the Hall rifle in the War of 1812, the gun was in service for more than twenty-five years. It was used in campaigns against Native Americans, the Mexican War, and also at the start of the Civil War.

Guns and Conquest

When Americans expanded westward in the early 1840s, particularly after the Mexican War (1846–1848), they took their guns with them. Settlers searching for land frequently used their firepower against Native American tribes. Some Native Americans were supplied with guns and could fight equally with the settlers. And so for a time, Native Americans were able to protect their lands and people from conquest. In time, however, so many settlers moved west that the Native Americans were conquered.

During the country's early expansion, Samuel Colt marketed his guns to settlers heading west. Colt developed the first successful repeating pistol and had it patented in England in 1835. He established a factory in Hartford, Connecticut, where he produced guns that were used in the Mexican War and the Civil War (1861–1865). He called his six-shooter the Peacemaker, and this gun became very famous. The Colt Peacemaker became the standard army pistol and was used by cowboys, frontiersmen, sheriffs, and outlaws.

Another popular gun was the derringer pistol, which was invented by Philadelphia gunmaker John Deringer. This gun had a short barrel and was accurate to six or seven feet. On April 14, 1865, John Wilkes Booth used this type of gun to assassinate President Abraham Lincoln.

During the 1840s and 1850s, a period of technological innovation, U.S. arms production increased. In the "Wild West," the violent sprees of outlaws such as Frank and Jesse James, the Dalton boys, and Billy the Kid often became tales of legend rather than reports of crime. The entertaining shows of expert sharpshooters Buffalo Bill and Annie Oakley also became very popular with the American public. The soil in which America's gun culture would grow was prepared for seeding.

Guns and Emancipation

By the mid-1800s, Americans became split on the issue of slavery. This difference of opinion divided the country and pitted Americans against Americans. The Civil War resulted in thousands of citizens being armed and commissioned to fight. The weapon most commonly used in the war was the rifled musket. The musket was loaded with a cone-shaped bullet called a minié ball, which had been invented in 1849 by French army captain Claude Minié. When the musket was fired, the ball expanded and spiraled in the rifling. The rifled musket could be fired two times a minute, which added speed to accuracy as advantages over other guns at that time.

A decade later, this weapon was replaced with the breechloader, which was loaded from the breech located behind the barrel. A few of these new weapons were used on an experimental basis during the Civil War.

Another weapon developed during the Civil War was a ten-barreled, hand-cranked, quick-firing gun. Dr. Richard Gatling developed this weapon, which was able to fire eight hundred shots per minute by turning a crank handle. The Union Army did not readily adopt the Gatling gun. Instead, the army made its first order near the end of the war, and none were delivered until the fighting was over.

A wounded soldier keeps his gun close at hand. The Civil War pitted Americans against Americans and led to gun ownership as part of the country's cultural identity.

The Civil War changed the nation's attitude toward guns and killing. After the Civil War, some people began to view guns as part of their cultural identity and as something that made them better individuals and better patriots.[1] At the end of the war in 1865, the Union and Confederate armies allowed soldiers to take their firearms home with them.

Although the war was over, firearms production levels remained high while prices dropped. It soon became possible for nearly anyone to own a gun.[2] In May 1874, the *Wichita Eagle* reported that "Pistols are as thick as blackberries."[3] The seeds of America's gun culture were now planted, and they would soon grow and spread.

Guns and American Culture

By the middle of the 1870s, guns seemed to be everywhere—in homes, theaters, literature, art, music, and patriotic parades. The gun had become a fixed part of Americans' identification and culture.[4] Yet many Americans were not skilled in shooting firearms.

The National Rifle Association (NRA) was founded on November 17, 1871, to educate people about marksmanship and gun safety. The organization was formed by two Union veteran soldiers—Colonel William Conant Church and General George Wood Wingate. In 1872, the NRA purchased land for a target-shooting range in Long Island, New York. One year later, the range, called Creedmoor, opened and began to host annual shooting matches. The NRA, a pro-gun group, continues to promote firearms training and education.

The development of guns continued, and the weapons became more deadly. In 1885, Hiram Maxim invented the first machine gun that did not have to be cranked by hand. Several years later, John Browning developed a machine gun called the Colt-Browning, which could fire four hundred rounds per minute.

In 1921, John Thompson invented the submachine gun that became nicknamed the tommy gun. This lightweight weapon weighed less than ten pounds, yet had the firepower of a machine gun. Before Thompson could sell his gun to the U.S. Army, a peace treaty was signed to end World War I.

Although the military no longer needed large numbers of guns, there were plenty of other customers for these small but powerful weapons. Many criminals purchased tommy guns during the era of Prohibition. In 1920, the Eighteenth Amendment was added to the U.S. Constitution. The Prohibition Amendment banned the manufacture, sale, or transport of alcoholic beverages. Many people, called bootleggers, ignored the law and made and distributed alcohol illegally. Bootleggers had many run-ins with the law, which frequently resulted in fierce shoot-outs.

Just like the Wild West gunslingers, bootleggers and professional criminals were often glamorized. Crime bosses Al Capone, John Dillinger, Bugs Moran, George "Machine Gun" Kelly, and Pretty Boy Floyd became well known to the American public. On the other side of the law, agent Eliot Ness of the Federal Bureau of Investigation (FBI) earned his reputation tracking down and arresting criminals during the Prohibition Era. He and his fellow agents earned the nickname "the Untouchables" because they could not be bribed or scared off by the organized crime rings. Prohibition was abolished in 1933; by this time, the tommy gun had become a symbol of organized crime.

Guns played a role in American culture during the rest of the twentieth century—particularly during World War II, the Korean War, the Vietnam War, student and civil rights protests, political assassinations, and rising urban crime, including violent acts of gangs or drug lords. In fact, guns have been a part of America throughout its history. Guns have been used by many Americans— settlers and soldiers, law officers and criminals, and hunters and target-shooting enthusiasts—for many reasons. By 2001, NRA membership had grown to more than 4 million people.[5] The organization is currently a powerful voice for gun enthusiasts. However, it faces strong opposition from various gun control organizations that are concerned with the negative impact of guns on society.

Gun control first began being publicly debated in the 1920s and 1930s, as gun violence became a social concern during the Prohibition Era. Today, gun violence is still a serious social problem. Yet guns remain a part of American culture. How much of a part they should play is still being debated.

*G*uns are examined in a guard room in England in 1944. Soldiers have been trained to use guns to protect their countries' interests throughout history.

Chapter 3

Regulation of Gun Ownership and Use

The Second Amendment to the
United States Constitution declares:

> *A well regulated Militia, being necessary to the*
> *security of a free State, the right of the people to*
> *keep and bear Arms, shall not be infringed.*

Some people interpret this amendment to mean that
all U.S. citizens have the *individual* right (a right belonging
to each and every person) to bear arms. Other people
interpret this amendment to mean that U.S. citizens as a
group have the *collective* right (a right belonging to people
as a group) to bear arms, especially in the context of a
militia. Each phrase of this amendment is interpreted dif-
ferently by groups supporting and opposing gun control.
People disagree about the definition of "a well regulated
Militia." They also question which people should bear
arms and which arms they should be able to bear.

An important legal case regarding the Second
Amendment was *United States* v. *Miller* (1939). The law-
suit challenged the National Firearms Act of 1934
discussed later in this chapter. After the firearms act
became law, Jack Miller and Frank Layton were arrested
for going from Oklahoma to Arkansas while carrying a
sawed-off, or shortened, shotgun. The 1934 law made

this act illegal. In its ruling, the Court noted that this weapon was not usual military equipment. Justice James C. McReynolds stated the Court's support of the federal government to regulate firearms. He also clearly stated that citizens possess a constitutional right to bear arms only in connection with service in a militia.[1]

United States v. *Miller* continues to play an important role in deciding the legality of gun control laws.

State Gun Control Laws and Legal Rulings

Throughout much of the nation's history, the federal government did not act to control gun use. Instead, it left regulation of guns to state and local governments. Most state constitutions guarantee the right to bear arms. However, most states have also acted to limit gun ownership and use at one time or another. Some early state gun laws aimed at preventing African Americans—both free and slave—from possessing firearms. Other examples of state gun control laws follow.

In 1911, New York State passed the Sullivan Law, which required a police permit to possess a handgun. Nearly a century later, New York is still the only state that significantly restricts private ownership of handguns.[2] The Sullivan Law was the first law that the NRA, a pro-gun organization, lobbied against. However, at the time, it did not have enough political clout to defeat the bill.[3]

Seventy years later, on June 8, 1981, the village of Morton Grove, Illinois, banned the possession of handguns, except by police, prison officials, the military, gun collectors, and others needing guns for their work. However, residents who owned guns could keep and use them in licensed gun clubs. The NRA and other gun enthusiasts challenged this law. Two courts ruled that the Second Amendment did not apply to the states and that there was no individual right to bear arms. The case, *Quilici* v. *Village of Morton Grove*, was appealed to the U.S.

Supreme Court, which declined to hear it. This meant that the ruling of the lower federal courts was upheld.

Federal Gun Control Laws

During the 1920s and 1930s, in the Prohibition Era, the U.S. government expanded its police powers. As the black market for illegal alcohol grew, the federal government became the primary force to combat the bootleggers. The FBI, the Federal Bureau of Narcotics, and the U.S. Border Patrol were all founded during this era.

When guns became more common in criminal activities, the government as well as other groups began passing laws that restricted their use. In 1922, the American Bar Association, an organization made up of lawyers, called for a ban on the manufacture and sale of pistols except for government use. In 1927, Congress passed a law banning shipment of handguns to individuals by the U.S. Post Office. However, gun manufacturers frequently skirted this law by sending guns to customers using private shippers.

With the election of President Franklin D. Roosevelt in 1932 came the first focused effort of the federal government to control gun ownership and use.[4] The National Firearms Act was passed in 1934. Its main purpose was to prevent automatic weapons from being used on American streets. The law targeted sawed-off shotguns and machine guns, which were among the main weapons used by organized crime groups during that time. In addition, a two hundred dollar tax was added to all gun sales.

Another federal gun control law passed by Congress was the Federal Arms Act of 1938. This law was aimed at those people involved in selling and shipping guns between different states and other countries. Anyone who sold a gun was required to obtain a Federal Firearms License for a one dollar annual fee. The law also prohibited selling guns to someone convicted of a serious crime, or felony, or to a criminal running from the law.

The next significant gun control law, and the most important national regulation, was passed in 1968. In the 1960s, three assassinations shocked the nation. On November 22, 1963, President John F. Kennedy was assassinated as he rode in a motorcade through the streets of Dallas, Texas. The man who shot him, Lee Harvey Oswald, used a rifle that he purchased through the mail.[5] On April 4, 1968, in Memphis, Tennessee, James Earl Ray assassinated civil rights leader Martin Luther King, Jr. And just two months after this tragic murder, Sirhan Bishara Sirhan assassinated presidential candidate Robert F. Kennedy after the young senator gave a campaign speech in Los Angeles, California. Once again, the American public became vocal about gun violence.

The Gun Control Act of 1968 restricted the sale of handguns over state lines and banned mail order sales of rifles and shotguns. It also banned the importation of handguns from other countries. In addition, more gun dealers were required to become licensed and were prohibited from selling firearms or ammunition to certain people. Dealers could not sell guns to minors, criminals, illegal aliens, drug addicts, and those with a mental illness. The law also set additional penalties for those who used a firearm when they committed a crime.

The Gun Control Act of 1968 was the strongest measure that had yet been passed.[6] However, there were several loopholes in this law. One way gun dealers got around the ban on importing handguns was to import handgun parts. Then they would assemble the entire weapon in the United States. Thus, despite the law's attempt to get tough on guns, small arms were still readily available to individuals.

In the early 1970s, when it became clear that people were using loopholes in the Gun Control Act of 1968, other gun control bills were introduced to Congress. However, the topic of gun control was a hot one. So gun control bills were often quickly tabled or sent through the red tape of committee procedures.[7]

*S*hown here are President John F. Kennedy and his wife, Jacqueline, arriving in Dallas, Texas, on November 22, 1963. Later that day, the president was killed by a bullet from an assassin's rifle.

In 1972, the Bureau of Alcohol Tobacco and Firearms (BATF) was created from the Treasury's Alcohol and Tobacco Tax Division of the Internal Revenue Service. The organization renamed itself by replacing "Tax" with "Firearms." The BATF nearly doubled in size and became responsible for enforcing the Gun Control Act of 1968.

The next important gun control law to be passed was the Firearms Owners' Protection Act of 1986. It was the first major reform of federal firearm laws since 1968. This law, also known as the Gun Control Act of 1986, eased restrictions on gun sellers and the sale of rifles and shotguns. It also permitted gun dealers to sell firearms in places other than their stores, such as at gun shows.

Another law, the Undetectable Firearms Act of 1988, made it illegal to make, import, or sell plastic guns. Guns made of plastic can be smuggled past metal detectors in places such as airports.

On March 30, 1981, John F. Hinckley, Jr., who was later diagnosed with a mental illness, tried to assassinate President Ronald Reagan. President Reagan was shot in the chest, but surgeons were able to remove the bullet, and he made a full recovery. However, three other people were shot, including Reagan's press secretary, James S. Brady. Brady was seriously wounded and today is still confined to a wheelchair. He can walk only a few steps without help. After a long recovery period, he can now help his wife, Sarah, in her national campaign for gun control. Sarah Brady began pushing for gun regulation shortly after Hinckley shot her husband. The law she campaigned for, called the Brady Bill, required background checks and waiting periods for people buying handguns from federally licensed gun dealers. Law enforcement officers performed background checks by investigating a gun buyer's personal history. For example, officers would check to see if the buyer had ever been convicted of a crime. In addition, gun buyers were required to wait a certain amount of time between requesting to buy a gun and receiving the weapon. This has become known as the "waiting period."

During the 1980s, another shooting captured the public's attention. On December 22, 1984, Bernhard Goetz was approached by four young men while riding a New York City subway. The four surrounded Goetz and demanded money. Goetz, who had been robbed in the past, thought he was going to be beaten and robbed again. So he pulled out a handgun and fired. He wounded all four and then fled the scene and the state. Goetz did return to stand trial in New York, and the media covered its every detail. Some people supported Goetz, while

*P*olice and Secret Service agents wrestle with assailant John Hinkley, Jr., while White House press secretary James Brady lies wounded on the sidewalk outside a Washington hotel in 1981.

others thought he was a dangerous vigilante, or self-appointed crime fighter. There was much controversy around the case, called *The People* v. *Bernhard Goetz*. In the end, Goetz was acquitted of the shooting charges and convicted on a lesser charge of illegal possession of a firearm.

The Crime Control Act passed in 1990 directed the U.S. attorney general to develop a strategy for establishing "drug-free school zones." The law also included criminal penalties for anyone possessing or firing a gun in a school zone.

In 1993, the Brady Handgun Violence Prevention Act was finally passed. It required a waiting period before an individual could buy a gun. Gun buyers had to complete a form, which state and local police would then use to check the individual's background. The Brady Law went into effect on February 28, 1994. It took so long to pass because of the heated debate between pro- and anti-gun control groups.[8]

The Violent Crime Control and Law Enforcement Act of 1994, commonly called the "assault weapons ban," was passed in 1994. This law made it illegal to manufacture, possess, or import new semiautomatic assault weapons for civilian use. Another law passed in 1994 was the Youth Handgun Safety Act. This law also prohibited the possession of handguns by anyone under eighteen years of age. People who sold handguns to minors could be sentenced to jail for up to ten years.

In 1997, the U.S. Supreme Court ruled 5–4 that the Brady Law was unconstitutional for violating the Tenth Amendment. (The Tenth Amendment gives states powers not delegated or prohibited by the U.S. Constitution.) The Court found that Congress had overstepped its power by making state and local officials help put a federal law into effect without receiving pay or funding for their effort. Until this ruling, state and local police officers had been required to perform the background checks on individuals buying guns. Now they were no longer forced to do so. The Supreme Court did not strike down the waiting period provision of the law.

On November 30, 1998, the National Instant Criminal Background Check System (NICS) was put into operation by the FBI. Gun dealers must contact this national background system before selling a gun to a customer. The purpose of the background check is to ensure that customers are legally eligible to buy a gun.

Major Federal Laws on Gun Control	
Name of Law	**Year passed**
National Firearms Act	1934
Federal Arms Act	1938
Gun Control Act	1968
Firearms Owner's Protection Act	1986
Undetectable Firearms Act	1988
Crime Control Act	1990
Brady Handgun Violence Prevention Act	1993
Violent Crime Control and Law Enforcement Act	1994
Youth Handgun Safety Act	1994

U.S. Government versus U.S. Citizens

While the government has a responsibility to protect its citizens, it also needs to respect the right of individuals. In the 1990s, government law enforcement officers faced off against U.S. citizens in two well-publicized incidents. The first occurred in Ruby Ridge, Idaho, and the second took place in Waco, Texas.

Randy Weaver was a follower of Christian Identity, an extremist religious group that believed white people were God's chosen people.[9] He lived in a cabin with his family and friend Kevin Harris on Ruby Ridge in northern Idaho. Agents from the BATF wanted information about several groups that Weaver was associated with. So the agents set up a situation in which an informant for the BATF bought sawed-off shotguns from Weaver. After refusing to act as a BATF informant himself, Weaver was charged with the crime of selling sawed-off shotguns. Months later, Weaver was arrested without a struggle, charged, and released on bail. When he broke the law by refusing to appear in court, agents of the U.S. Marshal's Service surrounded his cabin and began watching his activity.

On August 21, 1992, gunfire was exchanged between

the two groups as Weaver, his teenage son Sammy, and Harris walked in the woods around the cabin. During the quick exchange of bullets, a U.S. marshal and Weaver's son and dog were killed. In a later exchange of gunfire, a federal agent shot and killed Weaver's wife, Vicki, as she stood in the doorway of the cabin holding her infant daughter. On August 30, Harris, who was badly wounded, came out of the cabin. One day later, the rest of the family surrendered to the federal agents.

In a trial lasting thirty-six days, Weaver was found

*C*onfiscated guns and ammunition are displayed for members of the media and FBI agents outside the home of Randy Weaver in Naples, Idaho, in 1992.

guilty on two charges: failing to appear in court and violating his bail conditions.[10] In terms of the shootings, the jury ruled that Weaver and Harris acted in self-defense in firing at the federal agents.

About six months after the first shot was fired at Ruby Ridge, another violent confrontation between the U.S. government and American citizens occurred.[11] On February 28, 1993, FBI and BATF agents found themselves in a gun battle with residents at a Branch Davidian compound in Waco, Texas. Before the shoot-out took place, the Branch Davidians, a small religious group led by David Koresh, were charged with possession of unregistered machine guns and hand grenades. Government agents also received reports of possible child abuse. For fifty-one days, the religious group and BATF agents were locked in a stalemate.

On February 28, residents of the compound were told to leave or they would be exposed to tear gas. Some left, but eighty-three followers of Koresh stayed with their leader. In the gun battle that followed, four agents and several members of the Branch Davidians died, including Koresh. In addition, a fire broke out, adding to the mayhem and confusion and increasing the numbers of those who were seriously injured and killed.

Both these violent confrontations are filled with controversy and conflicting information. However, people can agree on one fact: The violent shoot-outs added ammunition for both sides of the gun control debate.

Who Is Ultimately Responsible for Gun Violence?

The next violent incident to escalate the gun control debate involved young people. The tragic Columbine High School shooting in 1999 renewed arguments about people's need for and use of guns. People also started to ask who should be held responsible for gun injuries and deaths. Should adults be responsible for children who misuse their guns? Should gun manufacturers be responsible for customers who purchase their guns and then use them to commit crimes?

The twentieth century closed and the twenty-first century began with numerous lawsuits against gun manufacturers. Cities, counties, and individuals filed the lawsuits, which were based on theories of industry negligence, or carelessness. This mass legal action followed the same strategy as that of state and local government lawsuits against the tobacco industry.[12] Both the tobacco and gun industries were being held accountable for injuries and deaths and ordered to make payments to cover physical and mental damages.

In 1999, a Brooklyn, New York, jury held several gun manufacturers responsible for a shooting based on the way the company had marketed its products. It was the only legal finding of its kind in the country.[13] Two years later, in 2001, an appeals court ruled that the gun industry cannot generally be held liable for shootings involving guns bought and sold illegally.[14]

Today, the gun control issue is still a "hot potato." The next two chapters outline the gun control arguments that people and politicians toss back and forth.

Chapter 4

Arguments in Favor of Gun Control

Many people who are in favor of gun control laws point to the grave injury and needless deaths, particularly among young people, that often result from guns. They claim that guns are not necessary possessions for the average American citizen in the twenty-first century. The following headings list some of the arguments made by people who are in favor of gun control.

Argument #1:
Gun Ownership and Use Is Not Guaranteed by the U.S. Constitution

People who favor gun control believe that the Second Amendment does not guarantee the right to bear arms to all citizens. In fact, they point out that the U.S. Constitution does not mention a citizen's right to bear arms beyond the purpose of participating in a militia.

Many constitutional scholars have also interpreted the Second Amendment's purpose to be providing arms to the population for the nation's defense. Over the years, the U.S. Supreme Court has generally allowed federal and state governments to regulate gun ownership and use.

Argument #2:
Gun Violence Is a Serious Social Problem

Many supporters of gun control point to the regulation of firearms as a way to reduce violence caused by guns, particularly in schools. The school gun violence that occurred during the first week of March 2001 offers tragic evidence of how guns are a serious problem in today's society.

The United States has a higher murder rate than many other countries. The following table lists the number of people murdered by handguns in the United States in 1996.[1] The number is significantly more than in countries such as Canada and Japan.

1996 International Comparison of Homicides Using Handguns	
Country	Number of Deaths
New Zealand	2
Japan	15
Great Britain	30
Canada	106
United States	9,390

Research by the FBI indicated that more than half, about 66 percent, of all murders in 2000 were committed with a gun.[2]

Argument #3:
Guns Increase the Risk of Suicide and Accidental Shootings

In 1998, nearly three of every five suicides (57 percent) were committed with a gun.[3] In addition, numerous accidental gun shootings occur every year. In 1994, there were more than thirteen hundred accidental deaths related to guns.[4] Many accidental gun shootings involve young people finding and playing with guns, as noted in

Chapter 1. Other deaths and injuries are related to hunting.

The following table lists the number of U.S. gun deaths from murders, suicides, and accidents during the 1981–1999 period.[5]

U.S. Gun Deaths from 1981 to 1999			
Year	Murders	Suicides	Accidents
1981	15,089	16,139	1,871
1982	13,830	16,560	1,756
1983	12,040	16,600	1,695
1984	11,815	17,113	1,668
1985	11,836	17,363	1,649
1986	13,029	18,153	1,452
1987	12,657	18,136	1,440
1988	13,645	18,169	1,501
1989	14,464	18,178	1,489
1990	16,218	18,885	1,416
1991	17,146	18,526	1,441
1992	17,488	18,169	1,409
1993	18,253	18,940	1,521
1994	17,527	18,765	1,356
1995	15,551	18,503	1,225
1996	14,037	18,166	1,134
1997	13,252	17,566	981
1998	11,789	17,424	866
1999	10,828	16,599	824

Although gun deaths are declining, the numbers are still very large. People in favor of gun control believe that these numbers could be sharply lowered by passing stricter gun control laws.

Argument #4:
Guns Escalate Violence

The Columbine school shooting, as well as many other gun-related deaths, shows how guns can increase the level of violence during a confrontation. Small arguments

*P*eople in favor of gun control argue that stricter gun laws will lower shooting-related deaths.

can turn deadly if a person decides to settle the disagreement using a gun.

The Centers for Disease Control and Prevention recently worked with the U.S. Justice and Education departments on a study of violent deaths at American schools. The study found that although the number of violent deaths at American schools is dropping, in a growing number of cases, the violent outbursts are claiming more than one life.[6] This finding indicates that guns can increase not only the level of violence in a conflict, but also the number of deaths.

Young people are not the only ones who reach for a gun during a confrontation. Many adults use guns to try to solve household and neighborhood arguments as well as disputes while driving. A study sponsored by the AAA Foundation for Traffic Safety found that aggressive driving and road rage have been steadily increasing during the 1990s. In fact, firearms are one of the most commonly used weapons in incidents of road rage.[7]

Argument #5:
Guns Create a False Sense of Security

Many people buy a gun to use for self-defense from intruders in their home or from criminals on the street. However, having a gun does not protect people from crime or from being shot themselves. In fact, having a gun at home may increase the possibility of a gun injury or death rather than that of saving a life.

According to a 1998 study by the *Journal of Trauma*, a gun kept in a home is twenty-two times more likely to kill a family member or friend than an intruder.[8] Also, using a gun to resist a violent attack can actually increase a person's risk of being injured or killed.[9] Indeed, most people tend to hesitate or freeze up when faced with a life-threatening or traumatic situation. On the other hand, criminals with guns rarely hesitate to fire their weapons. In fact, some intruders may be more likely to shoot a victim who is pointing a gun at them. Also, intruders may be able to take a gun and turn the table on those trying to protect themselves.

Argument #6:
Gun Injuries Cost Taxpayers Money

By the 1990s, people started looking at gun violence as a public health issue in the same way that they viewed drug abuse problems.[10] In their book *Gun Violence: The Real Costs*, authors P. J. Cook and J. Ludwig reported on their study of the costs of gun violence. They estimated that the total cost of gun violence to the nation is $100 billion a year.[11] This estimate includes both direct and indirect costs, such as medical expenses, lost wages, and security costs. In fact, the average total cost of one gun crime can be as high as $1.79 million, including medical treatment and the prosecution and imprisonment of the shooter.[12] American taxpayers pay most of these enormous expenses.

Summary

In general, people who are in favor of gun control are said to have a "blame the weapons" view. This is because many supporters of gun control believe much of the gun-related injury and death in the United States can be reduced by strict gun control. In other words, if society makes guns harder to own and use in public, then gun deaths and injury will dramatically decline.

Federal as well as state and local governments do have gun control laws. In fact, according to the National Center for Policy Analysis, there are more than twenty thousand gun-control laws in the United States.[13] Some laws restrict who can own guns, particularly those most likely to misuse guns. High-risk gun owners include those with criminal records, those with substance abuse problems, and those with mental illnesses.

Other laws restrict types of guns that can be owned by civilians. High-risk guns are firearms that are more likely to be misused. These include machine guns, sawed-off shotguns, and assault weapons.

People who support gun control would like more and tougher regulations for buying, carrying, and firing a gun. Most supporters of gun control do not want to totally ban guns. They want to pass commonsense measures that keep guns out of criminals' and children's hands. However, there are people in the United States who disagree that the country needs stricter gun control laws or any more gun restrictions at all.

Chapter 5

Arguments Against Gun Control

Many people who are against gun control laws point to the Second Amendment of the U.S. Constitution. They claim that gun ownership is a constitutional right that should not be eliminated or restricted by federal, state, or local governments. The following headings list some of the arguments made by people who are against gun control.

Argument #1:
Gun Ownership and Use Is Guaranteed by the U.S. Constitution

People who are against gun control believe that the Second Amendment guarantees every American citizen the right to keep and bear arms. They point to the amendment's wording "the right of the people" as opposed to "the right of the state." Some people compare the right to own a gun with the right to free speech. They do not think people should have to register before exercising either of these American liberties. In fact, many people who are against gun control believe that gun ownership by citizens is a way to guarantee the nation's liberty and security.

Argument #2:
Gun Control Laws Do Not Stop Criminals

Opponents of gun control believe that gun laws do not really stop criminals from using guns. They point out that most criminals do not apply for a gun license and so do not undergo a background check or waiting period. Instead, criminals tend to get their guns from illegal or black market sources.

In their 1992 study *Myths About Gun Control*, Dr. Morgan O. Reynolds and W. W. Caruth III noted that "the places where gun control laws are toughest tend to be the places where the most crime is committed with illegal weapons."[1] The researchers pointed out that New York State, with one of the toughest gun laws in the nation, has 20 percent of the armed robberies in the country.[2]

*O*pponents of gun control contend that gun laws do not stop criminals from having guns and that responsible gun ownership, not tougher laws, would reduce accidental deaths.

In other words, gun enthusiasts believe that laws making it harder for people to get a gun legally do not stop criminals from getting weapons illegally. In fact, gun control laws may actually put law-abiding citizens at a disadvantage over criminals, as the gun laws make it harder for citizens to legally get a gun. Many people opposed to gun control believe that criminals will continue to inflict violence on society, with or without stricter gun control laws.

Argument #3:
Guns Are Needed for Self-Defense

Opponents of gun control believe that gun control laws might compromise the ability of honest citizens to defend themselves against an attack. They point to incidents in which people without guns have been seriously hurt or killed during an attack or other crime.

James Edward Scott, an eighty-three-year-old man, shot and wounded an intruder in his backyard in Baltimore, Maryland. According to his neighbors, Scott had been the victim of repeated burglaries. After this incident, they said, authorities took away Scott's gun. Less than a year later, someone again broke into Scott's house, but he did not have his gun. The police said that Scott was strangled when he confronted the burglar.[3]

Argument #4:
Guns Can Prevent Crime

According to people who oppose gun control, criminals are less likely to commit crimes if they know their victims are armed. In 1993, the media focused on a German tourist who was shot by young criminals at a rest area along Interstate 10 near Tallahassee, Florida. Producers of a television program visited juvenile detention facilities in south Florida to discover why violent juvenile offenders were targeting foreign tourists. The jailed juveniles said they knew that the tourists did not have guns.[4]

Prisoners in ten state correctional systems were interviewed. Of those surveyed, 56 percent claimed that they would not attack someone whom they knew had a gun.[5] In other words, more than half of the criminals interviewed would be less likely to attack people if they thought there was a chance that their victim was armed with a gun.

However, a 1999 analysis of crime information disagrees with the above survey. The Brady Center to Prevent Gun Violence found that allowing people to carry concealed handguns did not mean there would be less crime. In the twenty-nine states that had laws allowing people to carry concealed weapons, the crime rate fell 2.1 percent from 1996 to 1997. During the same period, crime fell 4.4 percent in the twenty-one states that had strict laws prohibiting people from carrying concealed weapons.[6]

Argument #5:
Gun Control Is Difficult to Enforce

Many gun enthusiasts point to the failure of Prohibition to stop the manufacture and distribution of alcohol as a reason to block gun control laws. Restrictions on alcohol use ended up creating black markets and organized crime. Prohibition is evidence of how difficult it is to regulate moral behavior. Some people who are opposed to gun control believe that strict gun control laws could lead to the development of more black markets for acquiring illegal weapons.

People against gun control claim that many gun control laws already in place are not strictly enforced. Many of those opposed to gun control believe that rather than passing new laws, current laws should be more strongly enforced. They wonder how new gun control laws will help solve the problem of gun violence that current laws have not affected.

Argument #6:
Gun Control Laws Can Discourage People from Acting Responsibly

Those who support individual gun ownership say that many responsible people own unregistered guns. For example, a store owner who has been robbed several times may want to acquire a gun as soon as possible for self-defense. To get the gun quickly, such a person may not obey gun control laws. Then this person, who is otherwise a law-abiding citizen, probably will not take the illegal gun to a target-shooting range to practice shooting. Gun owners who do not practice shooting their weapon or who do not attend safety classes are not acting responsibly. In this way, stricter gun control laws may actually encourage irresponsible purchase and gun use.

Some people find themselves in a situation in which they do not report a crime against them because they used a gun, legal or illegal, in self-defense. They fear that a criminal charge may be brought against them.

Pro-gun groups point to the following numbers about accidents involving firearms versus those involving cars. They note that deaths from gun accidents have declined while deaths from motor vehicle accidents have risen sharply.[7]

Accidental Death Statistics		
Year	Motor Vehicles	Firearms
1910	1,900	1,900
1920	12,500	2,700
1930	32,900	3,200
1940	34,501	2,375
1950	34,763	2,174
1960	38,137	2,334
1970	54,533	2,406
1980	53,172	1,955
1990	46,800	1,400

Summary

In general, people who are against stricter gun control laws are said to have a "blame the users" view. This is because many gun enthusiasts often state the NRA slogan: "Guns don't kill people; people kill people." Anti-gun control groups claim that individuals should take responsibility for how they act, including safely owning, storing, and using firearms. These groups do not see placing strict controls on gun ownership and use as solving society's gun problems.

Many people who are against passing more gun control laws believe that gun ownership is a constitutional right much as the freedom of speech is. Anti-gun control groups do not think that restricting gun ownership and use will automatically decrease crime and violence. These groups believe that responsible, law-abiding citizens should not be prevented from owning guns or forced to follow time-consuming or costly procedures to own or use guns.

So the gun debate continues. Who should be able to own and use guns? What guns should they be allowed to own and use? Who is responsible when guns are used to kill and maim?

Chapter 6

Gun Control in the Twenty-first Century

The gun control debate, indeed, is a controversial issue. Each side has strong beliefs about gun ownership and use. And each side works to build its case and win supporters. The emotional aspect of this issue causes information and facts to sometimes be misrepresented.

Because of the controversy that surrounds the gun control issue, politicians are very careful about when and how they express their views. Most Americans do have an opinion on this issue. A 2000 political survey measured Americans' opinions on gun control:[1]

- ✔ 81 percent believed gun control is an important issue

- ✔ 91 percent said there should be at least minor restrictions on gun ownership

- ✔ 57 percent claimed that there should be major restrictions or a ban on firearms

In general, Americans have indicated that they would like stricter gun control laws. Still, pro-gun groups remain very vocal. And politicians cannot afford to ignore the campaign donations these pro-gun groups, such as the NRA, make to their election.

Summary of Gun Control Debate

Pro-gun control arguments

1. Gun ownership and use is not guaranteed by the U.S. Constitution.
2. Gun violence is a serious social problem.
3. Guns increase the risk of suicide and accidental shootings.
4. Guns escalate violence.
5. Guns create a false sense of security.
6. Gun injuries cost taxpayers money.

Anti-gun control arguments

1. Gun ownership and use is guaranteed by the U.S. Constitution.
2. Gun control laws do not stop criminals.
3. Guns are needed for self-defense.
4. Guns can prevent crime.
5. Gun control is difficult to enforce.
6. Gun control can discourage people from acting responsibly.

Without a change in the current climate, the debate will continue. In the meantime, people for and against gun control feed each other's fears based on what has happened or what they think will happen if their side does not win. In the process, they feed the fears of the American public as well. What can be done to resolve this debate? A middle ground must be found between absolutely no guns and absolutely no gun control.

The first step in settling the debate is to see what both sides agree on. One such issue is that guns should be used safely and responsibly.

*G*un shops like these make weapons available for American citizens who want a gun for recreation, hunting, or self-defense.

Gun Safety

Gun safety and education was one of the original purposes for creating the NRA. In July 1988, this organization developed the Eddie Eagle Gun Safety Program, an elementary gun safety education program for children in kindergarten through sixth grade. The program is taught nationwide with a simple message of "No. Go. Tell." If children see a gun, they should stop, leave the area without touching the weapon, and go tell an adult.

The gun safety procedures below are taken from a variety of sources and are important for anyone handling a gun to follow. They are commonsense rules that should never be broken.

✔ **Assume all guns are always loaded.** A person should handle an empty gun with the same care as a loaded one. Not only will this procedure prevent accidental shootings, it will also reinforce the habit of handling a gun safely.

✔ **A person should keep their finger off the trigger until they are ready to shoot.** The trigger is not a place to rest the finger between shots. Instead, a person should rest their finger on the trigger guard or on the body of the gun just above the trigger, which is known as the "index position."

✔ **Know the target and what is beyond it.** Bullets ricochet and sometimes pass through objects. In fact, bullets can skip over water just like stones do. So when shooting, a person should always know how solid the target is and what is around and behind it. They certainly do not want to shoot in the direction of other people. It is important to think first, shoot second.

✔ **A person should never point a gun at anything they are unwilling to shoot.** Since a person cannot always be sure that a gun is empty of ammunition, they should never point it at a target that they really do not want to shoot—particularly a person. The gun should always be pointed in a safe direction. By following this procedure, a person will not cause any damage, injury, or death should the gun be fired accidentally.

✔ **A gun should be kept at the least level of readiness necessary.** This means that a gun should always be kept unloaded when it is stored. This means that safety devices should be used while holding or carrying the weapon.

In the area of gun safety, manufacturing and technology companies are helping. Gun owners can buy locks for guns or trigger blocks that must be removed before the gun can be fired. These safety devices help ensure that only an authorized person can use the gun. In addition, many types of "smart" guns are now being designed. These guns are personalized so that only their owners can fire them. Smart guns can help prevent accidental shootings and suicides by young people as well as shooting deaths and injuries from stolen guns.

Addressing Gun Violence

Another issue that both sides agree on is that gun violence needs to be addressed. In May 2001, President George W. Bush said, "In America today, a teenager is more likely to die from a gunshot than from all natural causes of death combined."[2] He added that this grim fact had "caused too many families to bury the next generation. And for all our children's sake, this nation must reclaim our neighborhoods and our streets."[3] His words were part of his administration's commitment of $550 million over two years to finance new prosecutors and new programs aimed at reducing gun-related violence. In addition, Attorney General John Ashcroft has said that he believed Congress could enact gun control laws.[4]

In fact, recognizing the government's right to regulate guns is another area of agreement between pro- and anti-gun control groups. The debate is about how much and

*T*om Mauser, who lost a son in the Columbine High School shooting, holds the microphone for James Brady as he reads a speech during a press conference for Project Exile in 2000.

what types of regulation the government should pass.[5] For example, the NRA, an organization of gun enthusiasts, supports government efforts to pass laws requiring licensing for carrying a concealed weapon. The NRA also approves of and financially supports Project Exile. Tough prosecution is the concept behind this crime-fighting strategy. Criminals who use guns to commit crimes are prosecuted in federal rather than state courts and face stiff penalties.

Moving Forward on the Gun Control Debate

By focusing on what they agree on, both sides of the gun control debate can move forward in addressing problems that result from the irresponsible use of guns. For example, both sides can focus on restricting gun ownership that is aimed at people with a history of violence and crime rather than at the general public. They can also amend current gun control laws to close any loopholes in enforcing these regulations. In addition, the two sides can be sure that people who use guns irresponsibly are given severe sentences.

The gun control debate may not be settled for quite some time. However, by understanding the issue—both the pros and cons—people can make better decisions about working toward a win-win solution.

The challenge is to balance law and order with personal freedom. Successful solutions to the gun control debate will be those that decrease gun crime and violence without unduly restricting the rights of responsible citizens.

Chapter 1. Youths and Guns

1. "Two Killed, 13 Hurt in Calif. High School Shooting," *Yahoo! News Canada*, March 5, 2001, <http://ca.news.yahoo.com/010305/5/36r9.html> (April 27, 2001).

2. "15 Injured in Calif. High School Shooting," *Rumor Mill News Reading Room Archive*, March 5, 2001, <http://www.rumormillnews.net/cgi-bin/archive.cgi?read=7274> May 6, 2002.

3. Ibid.

4. "San Diego Community Stunned by School Shooting," *The San Diego Channel*, March 6, 2001, <http://www.thesandiegochannel.com/sand/news/stories/news-52409720010305-110346.html> (May 18, 2001).

5. Todd S. Purdum, "Shooting at School Leaves 2 Dead and 13 Hurt," *The New York Times*, March 6, 2001, p. A1.

6. "Suspect in Shooting Rampage Charged with Two Murder Counts," *APBnews*, March 8, 2001, <http://www.apbnews.com/newscenter/breakingnews/2001/03/08/story_santana_shooting_01.html> (April 27, 2001).

7. Edward Wong, "Girl, 14, Arrested After a Classmate Is Shot in Pennsylvania," *The New York Times*, March 8, 2001, p. A20.

8. "More Guns, Violence Hit Schools," *Philadelphia Daily News*, March 8, 2001, <http://cofaxdn.philly.com/content/daily_news/2001/03/08/local/GUNN08.htm> (April 14, 2001).

9. Ibid.

10. "Firearm Facts," *Brady Campaign to Prevent Gun Violence Page*, n.d., <http://www.bradycampaign.org/facts/research/firefacts.asp> (December 11, 2001).

11. Ibid.

12. "Fatal Shootings Decline," *The New York Times*, April 13, 2001, p. A15.

13. Ibid.

14. "Gun-Related Death Rate Plummets," *The International Action Network on Small Arms Page*, November 1999, <http://www.iansa.org/news/1999/nov_99/guncdc.htm> (November 15, 2001).

15. "Crime and Gun Control," *National Center for Policy Analysis Idea House Page*, 2001, <http://www.ncpa.org/pi/crime/pd041301c.html> (November 15, 2001).

16. Jacob H. Fries, "Reach for Snack Turns Fatal as Girl, 9, Finds a Handgun," *The New York Times*, July 2, 2001, p. B3.

17. "Child Access Prevention (CAP) Laws and Gun Owner Responsibility Questions and Answers," *Brady Campaign to Prevent Gun Violence Page*, n.d., <http://www.bradycampaign.org/facts/issuebriefs/cap.asp> (April 9, 2002).

18. "Suicide in the United States," *National Center for Injury Prevention & Control Page*, n.d., <http://www.cdc.gov/ncipc/factsheets/suifacts.htm> (July 27, 2001).

19. Ibid.

20. "Organizing for a Safer America," *The Coalition to Stop Gun Violence Page*, n.d., <http://www.csgv.org/content/resources/resc_dyk.html> (December 6, 2001).

21. William J. Vizzard, *Shots in the Dark: The Policy, Politics, and Symbolism of Gun Control* (Lanham, Md.: Rowman & Littlefield Publishers, 2000), p. 14.

22. "NRA Hunter's Fact Card 1999," *NRA Headquarters Page*, n.d., <http://www.nrahq.org/shooting/hunting/huntfacts.asp> (July 17, 2001).

23. "The Self Defense Files: True Stories of Armed Self Defense for January, 2001," *Kentucky Coalition to Cary Concealed (KC3) Page*, February 1, 2001, <http://www.kc3.com/self_defense/armed_self_defense_jan_2001.htm> (May 24, 2001).

24. "Guns in the Home," *Brady Campaign to Prevent Gun Violence Page*, n.d., <http://www.bradycampaign.org/facts/issuebriefs/gunhome.asp> (April 9, 2002).

Chapter 2. The History of Gun Use

1. Jan E. Dizard, Robert Merrill Muth, and Stephen P. Andrews, Jr., *Guns in America: A Reader* (New York: New York University Press, 1999), p. 36.

2. Ibid.

3. Michael A. Bellesiles, *Arming America: The Origins of a National Gun Culture* (New York: Alfred A. Knopf, 2000), p. 430.

4. Ibid., p. 443.

5. "Heston Re-elected N.R.A. President," *The New York Times*, May 22, 2001, p. A17.

Chapter 3. Regulation of Gun Ownership and Use

1. Robert Emmet Long, ed., *Gun Control: The Reference Shelf*, vol. 60, no. 6 (New York: H. W. Wilson Company, 1989), p. 57.

2. William J. Vizzard, *Shots in the Dark: The Policy, Politics, and Symbolism of Gun Control* (Lanham, Md.: Rowman & Littlefield Publishers, 2000), p. 87.

3. Ibid., p. 88.

4. Ibid., p. 89.

5. Ibid., p. 94.

6. Long, p. 61.

7. Ibid., p. 63.

8. Wayne R. LaPierre, *Guns, Crime, and Freedom* (Washington, D.C.: Regnery Publishing, 1994), pp. 83–84.

9. Vizzard, p. 75.

10. LaPierre, p. 186.

11. Ibid., p. 190.

12. Vizzard, p. 81.

13. Richard Pérez-Peña, "State Court Sides with Gunmakers in Liability Case," *The New York Times*, April 27, 2001, p. A1.

14. Ibid.

Chapter 4. Arguments in Favor of Gun Control

1. "Firearm Facts," *Brady Campaign to Prevent Gun Violence Page*, n.d., <http://www.bradycampaign.org/facts/research/firefacts.asp> (December 11, 2001).

2. Bureau of Justice Statistics, "Summary Findings on Victimization," *U.S. Department of Justice Page*, n.d., <http://www.ojp.usdoj.gov/bjs/guns.htm> (April 27, 2001).

3. "Let's Put It into Perspective," *Project Gun Safety Page*, n.d., <http://www.cdc.gov/ncipc/factsheets/suifacts.htm> (July 25, 2001).

4. "Statistics: Death and Injury," *Gunfacts Page*, n.d., <http://www.gunfacts.org/accidental.htm> (July 29, 2001).

5. "Firearms Deaths in the United States, 1981–1999," *Brady Campaign to Prevent Gun Violence Page*, n.d., <http://www.bradycampaign.org/press/related_documents/1129a.pdf> (December 6, 2001).

6. "Multiple Slayings Now More Likely in School Violence," *The New York Times*, December 5, 2001, p. A25.

7. "Road Rage on the Rise, AA Foundation Reports," *U.S. Roads, Road Injury Prevention & Litigation Journal*, August 1999, <http://www.usroads.com/journals/rilj/9908/ri990803.htm> (December 12, 2001).

8. "Guns in the Home," *Brady Campaign to Prevent Gun Violence Page*, n.d., <http://www.bradycampaign.org/facts/issuebriefs/gunhome.asp> (April 9, 2002).

9. Franklin E. Zimring, "Firearms, Violence, and Public Policy," *Scientific American*, vol. 265, November 1991, pp. 48–54.

10. Osha Gray Davidson, *Under Fire: The NRA and the Battle for Gun Control* (New York: Henry Holt and Company, 1993), p. 281.

11. "Firearm Facts," *Brady Campaign to Prevent Gun Violence Page*, n.d., <http://www.bradycampaign.org/facts/research/firefacts.asp> (December 11, 2001).

12. Ibid.

13. "The Gun Control Controversy," *National Center for Policy Analysis Idea House Page*, May 12, 1999, <http://www.ncpa.org/pi/crime/pd051299d.html> (April 14, 2001).

Chapter 5. Arguments Against Gun Control

1. Robert W. Lee, "Shooting Down Faulty Arguments," *New American*, April 4, 1994, <http://www.thenewamerican.com/tna/1994/vol10no07.htm> (April 14, 2001).

2. Ibid.

3. John R. Lott, *More Guns, Less Crime* (Chicago, Ill.: The University of Chicago Press, 2000), pp. 12–13.

4. Wayne LaPierre, *Guns, Crime, and Freedom* (New York: HarperPerennial, 1995), p. 22.

5. Lott, p. 6.

6. "John Lott's More Guns, Less Crime: An Alternate Q&A," *Brady Campaign to Prevent Gun Violence Page*, n.d., <http://www.bradycampaign.org/facts/research/lott.asp> (December 11, 2001).

7. LaPierre, p. 63.

Chapter 6. Gun Control in the Twenty-first Century

1. "Issues Match: Absolute Right to Gun Ownership," *Isssues 2000 Page*, n.d., <http://www.issues2000.org/Frontline/im/q7.asp> (April 27, 2001).

2. Frank Bruni, "Citing the Drain of Violence, Bush Backs Increased Prosecution of Gun-Related Crimes," *The New York Times*, May 15, 2001, p. A16.

3. Ibid.

4. Fox Butterfield, "Broad View of Gun Rights Is Supported by Ashcroft," *The New York Times*, May 24, 2001, p. A19.

5. Lee Nisbet, ed., *The Gun Control Debate: You Decide* (Amherst, N.Y.: Prometheus Books, 2001), pp. 15–16.

Organizations Supporting Gun Control

Brady Center to Prevent Handgun Violence
1225 Eye Street, N.W., Suite 1100
Washington, D.C. 20005
(202) 289-7319

Coalition to Stop Gun Violence
1023 15th Street, N.W., Suite 600
Washington, D.C. 20005
(202) 408-0061

Mothers Against Violence in America
105 14th Avenue, Suite 2A
Seattle, WA 98122
(800) 897-7697

Violence Policy Center
1140 19th Street, N.W., Suite 600
Washington, D.C. 20036
(202) 822-8200

Organizations Opposing Gun Control

Citizen's Committee for the Right to Keep and Bear Arms (CCRKBA)
Liberty Park
12500 N.E. Tenth Place
Bellevue, WA 98005
(425) 454-4911

Gun Owners of America
8001 Forbes Place, Suite 102
Springfield, Virginia 22151
(703) 321-8585

National Rifle Association (NRA)
11250 Waples Mill Road
Fairfax, Virginia 22030
(703) 267-1000

Second Amendment Foundation
James Madison Building
12500 N.E. Tenth Place
Bellevue, WA 98005
(206) 454-7012

For More Information

Apel, Lorelei. *Dealing with Weapons at School and at Home.* New York: Powerkids, 1996.

Cozic, Charles P., ed. *Gun Control, Current Controversies.* San Diego, Calif.: Greenhaven Press, Inc., 1992.

Gottfried, Ted. *Gun Control.* Brookfield, Conn.: Millbrook Press, 1993.

Grapes, Bryan J. *School Violence.* San Diego, Calif.: Greenhaven Press, 2000.

Hanson, Freya Ottem. *The Second Amendment: The Right to Own Guns.* Springfield, N.J.: Enslow Publishers, Inc., 1998.

Klee, Sheila. *Working Together Against School Violence.* New York: Rosen Publishing Group, 1996.

Landau, Elaine. *Armed America: The Status of Gun Control.* Englewood Cliffs, N.J.: Julian Messner, 1991.

Schwarz, Ted. *Kids and Guns.* New York: Franklin Watts, 1999.

Shulson, Rachel Ellenberg. *Guns: What You Should Know.* Morton Grove, Ill.: A. Whitman, 1997.

Strahinich, Helen. *Think About Guns in America.* New York: Walker and Company, 1992.

Organizations Opposing Gun Control

Gun Owners of America
<http://www.gunowners.org>

National Rifle Association (NRA)
<http://www.nrahq.org>

Organizations Supporting Gun Control

Brady Center to Prevent Handgun Violence
<http://www.bradycenter.org>

Mothers Against Violence in America
<http://www.mavia.org>

Internet Addresses